LET'S FIND JOY!

SHAUNTI FELDHAHN
&
KATIE KENNY PHILLIPS

ILLUSTRATED BY
ANNABELLE GROBLER

ISBN: 978-0-578-88160-7

Printed in China

Authors: Shaunti Feldhahn & Katie Kenny Phillips

Illustrator: Annabelle Grobler

This book belongs to:

_____

_____

There's a treasure chest filled with something special! Is it rubies? Or diamonds? Or precious gold? No! It's something better by far! Jesus packed it full of JOY . . . and it's for you and for me—if only we will search for it!

But what is joy? Is it how we feel when we
jump in puddles? Or get a big hug? Or when
we've had a cookie or two? Well, those are
nice feelings but joy is much, much more
(it's like happiness times a million!)

Joy is when we have a smile deep down inside of us—
even when things feel hard or unfair or even a little
bit sad. If we know that God loves us and that
He's on our team, we can have joy! Always!

Let's go on a scavenger hunt to find this amazing treasure!
If we follow the map, and pay attention to the clues,
we'll figure out how to get there. Ready . . . set . . . GO!

The first clue on the map will make
us stop and say "WOW!"
It says, "God is a BIG God!"
Look outside and what do you see?
A sky and trees and flowers?
Do you hear birds? Or crickets?
God made them all!

Before moving on to
the next clue, let's say,
"God, You are a BIG God!
There's nothing You can't do!"
When we realize that God created everything in this great,
big, beautiful world, it helps us know He is in control!

The next clue tells us that one of the most important things we can learn to say is "Thank You!" It makes others feel good and it also makes our heart and brain feel happy, too. (It also means that when we feel grumpy about something, we need to stop ourselves and think of something we can say "thank you" for instead.)

PARTY

Before moving on to the
next clue, let's look at someone right now
and say "thank you" for something nice they
did for us today. And if we've been grumpy,
can we figure out a way to thank God for it
rather than grumbling?

Following the map, the next clue tells us two other things that matter: saying "I'm Sorry" and "I Forgive You." When we've hurt someone's feelings or do something that isn't kind, it's important to say we're sorry. And when someone apologizes to us, it's important to give them the gift of forgiveness. After all, God has forgiven us, and it makes us happy to be like Him.

Before moving on to the next clue, can you think of someone you need to say "I'm sorry" to? Someone you need to forgive? Let's practice saying, "I'm Sorry" and "I Forgive You." Pretend you are talking to that person. What will you say?

Next clue? It says, "Look Back!"
In order for us to move forward,
we need to look back at how God
has been with us our whole life.
He's kept us safe, given us good gifts
and made sure we have been loved
by Him and others. When we remind
ourselves that God takes care of us,
it gives us strength to take the next step,
and the next, and the next!

Before moving on to the next clue,
let's remember a time when God took good care of us.
Was it when we were sick?
Or when He answered a prayer?
Or when something really
amazing happened?

The next clue on our map says, "Believe Him!" We can't go anywhere on our scavenger hunt unless we believe God's clues. Our journey may go up and down and all around, but we need to trust He knows the way for us. It may not make sense to us, but God knows the WHOLE map! So we can believe Him that our next step is the right one!

Before moving on to the next clue,
can we think of a time that something happened
that didn't make sense but ended up being the exact right choice for us?
What might be happening right now that we just need to say,
"I believe you, God, that this is the next right step!"

THIS WAY

I PROMISE

TRUST ME

Okay . . . next clue!
It's one that tells us
to "Listen Carefully!"
Sometimes God uses a quiet voice
to tell us where to go or what to do.
Sometimes we have to get really quiet
to hear what God is saying. He uses the Bible
to talk to us. He also uses our parents
to help guide us.
The more we
practice listening,
the better we get
at knowing the next
step in the journey.

Before moving on to the next clue,
let's stop and get quiet.
It's important to ask God to help us
to listen and know what the next
right thing is for us.
Let's pray and say,
"God, help us listen carefully on this journey!"

We're almost there! The next clue reminds us to "Follow the Rules!" This one doesn't always feel so fun. We love to make up our own rules when we feel like they don't make sense. But God has guidelines for us to follow to keep us on track and headed in the right direction. When we follow God's rules, we can relax knowing we are safe and sound.

Before moving on to the last and final clue,
let's think of a rule our parents might have
that we don't always like to follow.
How does that rule work to keep us safe?
Let's think how the rules in our life are meant for our good!

Last clue! We're almost to the treasure!
It says we must "Help Others Along the Way!"
Our winding journey is not meant for us to do alone.
It's important to stop and help our friends and family
and even people we might not know along the way.
Helping others makes God happy,
so it makes our hearts happy as well.
That's a win-win because we're
all in this together!

Before moving on to the treasure,
can we think of someone we have helped?
How did it make them feel?
How did it make us feel?
Let's keep our eyes open to who God wants us to help next!
We've found all the clues! Now what do we do?

Let's review all the things
we've discovered along the map!

Clue #1: God is a BIG God

Clue #2: Say Thank You

Clue #3: Say I'm Sorry and I Forgive You

Clue #4: Look Back

Clue #5: Believe Him

Clue #6: Listen Carefully

Clue #7: Follow the Rules

Clue #8: Help Others Along the Way

Which ones are the easiest for us to do?
Which ones feel the hardest?
Remember, we can do hard things—
we're adventurers!
Are we ready to claim our treasure?

Here it is!
Our treasure chest . . . full of JOY!
Whenever we feel worried
or disappointed or scared—
or if we are happy or silly or glad
—joy is a treasure from God we can
have, ALWAYS! Jesus came to earth
to bring joy—no matter what is
going on around us!

Let's remember our clues
and share them with others.
Jesus wants us to share His treasure!
Because joy is not just for us—
but for everyone, everywhere.

"I bring you good news of great joy that will be for all the people."
(Luke 2:10 ESV)